Dedicated to my girls:
Arianna and Joanna.

Psalm 95:4-5
"In his hand are the depths of the earth, and the mountain peaks belong to him. The sea is his, for he made it, and his hands formed the dry land."

God created many animals, **BIG** and small, large and TALL, tiny and infinitesimal.

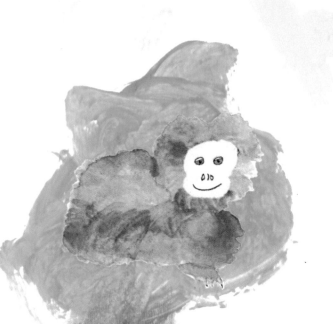

All animals God made of countless colors, from things that crawl on land, float under the sea, or fly high above **you** and me!

These animals may be grey, blue, or brown with many features.

But the animals this book talks about are the red creatures.

Where should we start to talk
about animals that are red?

How about we pick
the Fox, since it
can be said:
he is fast
and *sneaky* too.

What do you think about this **Red Fox**, can we find him in the zoo?

Mr. Fox has a thick coat that he uses to help keep warm.

He is a solitary creature; he does not live on a farm.

Let's talk about another red animal, Mrs. Red Panda.

She lives in the trees on the mountains of Nepal or Myanmar.

During the day she sleeps in those trees and doesn't go very far.

At night she goes out and forages for food. She munches on fruit and bamboo.

She can be very shy, as she is endangered.

If you see her in the wild, contact your local ranger.

Red Pandas and Foxes aren't very tall, but the Red Kangaroo is the largest marsupial of all.

Mr. Red Kangaroo hops along on his powerful hind limbs, those legs make him jump acting almost like springs.

Red Kangaroos

live on the Australian plains.
Here, Mr. Red Kangaroo lives
and remains.

When **Mr. and Mrs. Red Kangaroo** have a baby, it is called a joey.

A joey likes to bounce and play, but most of the time, in his momma's pouch he likes to stay.

The last red creature that this book will talk about is the most majestic and beautiful, no doubt.

The most magnificent red creature you may ever see is the Red Deer that live in Europe, Asia and Africa.
Don't you agree?

Mrs. Red Deer tends to not like to stay very still, so she migrates in summer to the top of the hill.

In winter she migrates back down to lower, woodier terrain, because the trees help to block the wind and the rain.

There are many more **red animals** that God has created. However, we cannot discuss them all in this book, it is not fated.

Just go outside and look around, there are many **red creatures** to be found!

Depending on where you live you could see the beautiful Red Cardinal flitting around,

or the Red Monkey swinging in the trees that abound.

Maybe you would notice the Red Squirrels that squeak, or even the Red Tailed Hawk who is not meek.

The important thing to remember is that we are all God's creatures, with all our different features.

Don't forget that God loves you very much, for in the world another one of you, there is nonesuch.

You were created to walk and talk with Him.

God made you special from the top of your head, to the bottom of your limbs.

He loves every one of his creations, but especially you.

You have a special purpose and can do anything you put your mind to.

If there's one thing from this book you should remember...

Know that God's love for you will last forever!

THE

END

Made in the USA
Columbia, SC
02 September 2022

66575221R00015